Through Him all things were made; without Him nothing was made that has been made.

John 1:3

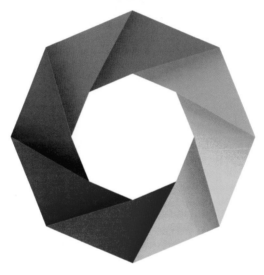

To find out more about how to know God, book updates and information or to purchase your own copy visit www.GodMadeColor.com

Scriptures taken from the Holy Bible, New International Version®, NIV®. Copyright © 1973, 1978, 1984, 2011 by Biblica, Inc.™ Used by permission of Zondervan. All rights reserved worldwide. www.zondervan.com The "NIV" and "New International Version" are trademarks registered in the United States Patent and Trademark Office by Biblica, Inc.™

ISBN: 0692524886
ISBN-13: 978-0692524886

Printed in the United States of America

GOD made color

written and illustrated by
jennifer burrell

God Made Black

To color the heavens in the night time sky
to show the power of a train speeding by
for bugs and reptiles that creep and crawl
But the most important thing of all

Is God made black to let us know
without His light our sin will grow
and when God's law, we disobey
there is a price that must be paid

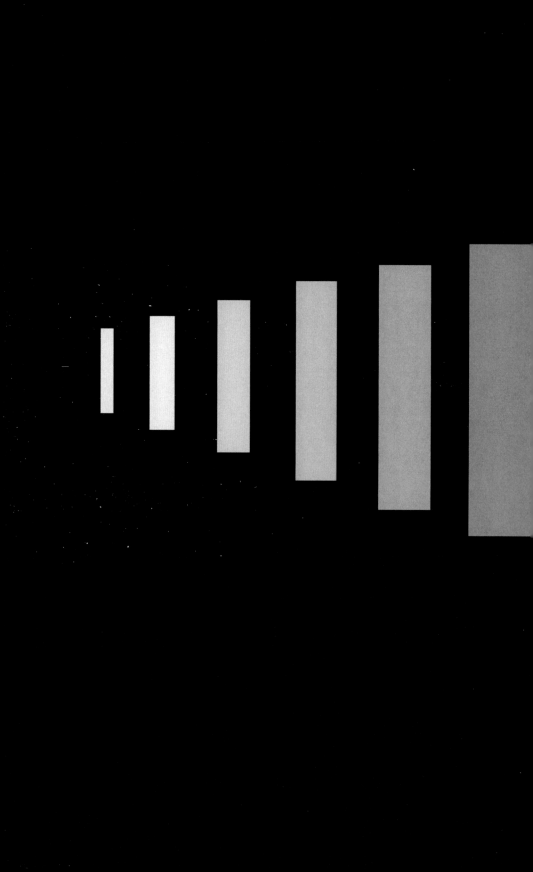

God Made Red

To show the beauty of a sweet scented rose
to warn of a fire engine with it's giant water hose
for juicy ripe apples to munch in the fall
but the most important thing of all

Is God made red to let us know
He sent His perfect Son to die and show
His unending love upon the cross
Christ's blood was shed, He paid our cost

If we confess our sins He is faithful and just and will forgive us our sins and purify us from all unrighteousness. I John 1:9

God Made White

To color winter with fresh fallen snow
for fresh clean shirts hung out in a row
for little lambs so sweet and small
but the most important thing of all

Is God made white to let us know
He will make your heart clean, His word tells us so
Admit you're a sinner and believe on His name
Tell others about how His child you became

Come near to God and He will come near to you.   James 4:8

God Made Green

To color His creation with living things
for fruits and veggies and butterfly wings
for a pod of peas and trees so tall
but the most important thing of all

Is God made green to let us know
Once you know Jesus, it's time to grow
Closer to your Savior everyday
By reading God's Word and learning to pray

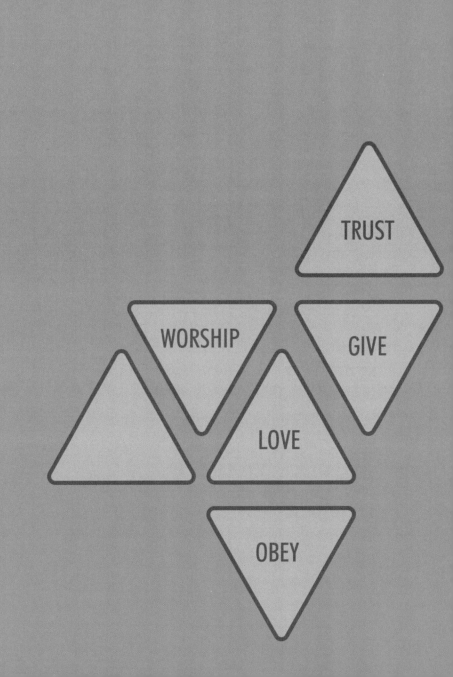

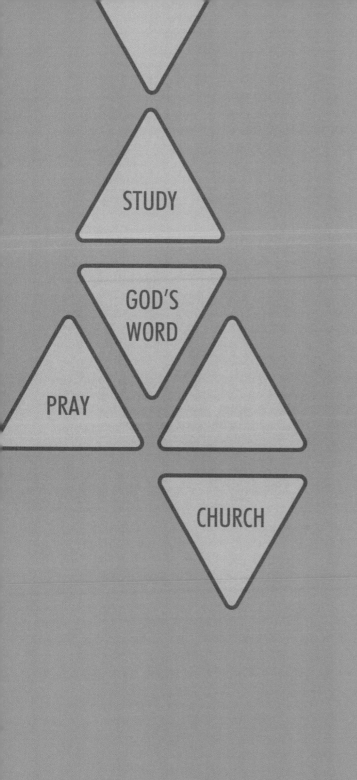

If I go and prepare a place for you, I will come back and take you to be with me that you also may be where I am. John 14:3

God Made Yellow

To color the sun that brightens our day
for daisies and daffodils blooming in May
for bright booming fireworks that sparkle and fall
but the most important thing of all

Is God made yellow to let us know
There's a home in heaven, where one day we will go
Christ lives today and prepares a place
He will return, we'll see His face

LIVE

Forever

dear parent,

If you ever went to Vacation Bible School as a child, you will probably remember a little craft project called the "wordless book". This tiny construction paper masterpiece was intended to help you easily share the gospel of Jesus Christ through the symbol of color. The concept has remained popular through the years, being incorporated into beaded bracelets and beach balls. The simple idea can be affordably reproduced and crosses language barriers. The format allows you to incorporate your own words or story. For some people that aspect of the wordless book can be a little intimidating. What did this color mean? What was I supposed to say here? Which Bible verse represented this color?

God Made Color is a simple rhyme based on the colors first introduced in the wordless book. Each color is accompanied by a verse from the Bible that supports the meaning behind the color. The illustrations provide silly and fun conversation starters to tell your children about the beauty of God's creation. But the most important thing of all....is God Made Color will introduce your young child to the message of the gospel. It is never too early to tell your child about God's love for them, even if they are not quite ready to fully understand it yet. Now what? Pray for your children. The God who is everywhere, knows everything and has all the power created and cares about you and your child. Pray that God will one day bring your child into a real relationship with Him in His perfect timing. I pray that God Made Color will become a fun and enjoyable tool to add to your family library and that it will provide opportunity to spend some time reading and playing with the little ones in your life.

Jennifer